Persevere:
Never Give Up

Zachary Corrothers

DEDICATION

This poetry series is dedicated to my dad, John Corrothers, a man of great wisdom and cancer survivor. Other acknowledgements are extended to the family members and friends who gave consistent support to see this dream into fruition. Many people across the globe have faced various forms of obstacles and unfortunate circumstances. This series has been created to be a great tool or resource to add any motivation and encouragement needed to finish each day. As things may not always go in your favor, it is up to each and every one of us to believe that we possess the keys to achieve success inside our hearts. We must not be discouraged when others or circumstances out of our control are not in our favor. We must continue to have good intentions in our hearts and be willing to always treat each other with respect.

CONTENTS

ACKNOWLEDGMENTS

Acknowledgements are as follows: John Corrothers, Heather Corrothers, Ty'Leyah Ross, Maurice Harris III, Andre Coleman, Desiree Coleman, Ryan Adkins, Robin Adkins, Daryl Howard, Phillip Holmes, Kenneth R. Elston V, Richard Shane Sames, Everett Hall, Jason Clarke, Jarryn Avery, and Jacob Frias.

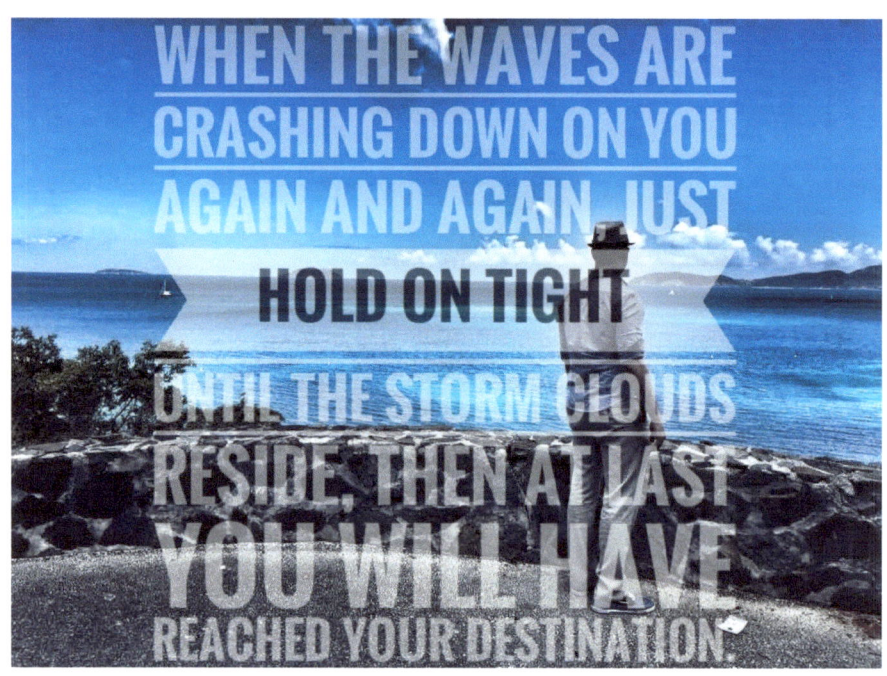

WHEN THE WAVES ARE CRASHING DOWN ON YOU AGAIN AND AGAIN, JUST HOLD ON TIGHT UNTIL THE STORM CLOUDS RESIDE, THEN AT LAST YOU WILL HAVE REACHED YOUR DESTINATION.

MY REACH

The race for success
Is one big test
It ain't for the mass
All it takes is a different class
You gotta be stout
To handle all the haters' shouts
Press on through all the crowds
Wait to hear the words that you have vowed

This is the road less traveled
Ever wonder why there are no flaws in the gravel
And the only way to find it is through failure
Trial and error is in our human nature
There are no road signs in order to survive
Just your inner drive
That will lead you to that light
You've had in sight

Success is not measured by wins and losses
But by how you overcome all of what life tosses,
Trying to break you down
In, out, and around
So don't let yourself be diverted
But always stay fully alerted
For other roads will cross your path
Just remember to always do the simple math

Work will get harder and tougher
Until you shine like the diamond in the rough dirt
You cannot be afraid to get cut
Or you'll never make the final cut
Soon your followers will bring home all the titles
And you'll become a legacy entitled
Then with your last breath, you can let out a victory shout
Cuz' you will have reached your success.

-Zachary Corrothers

FROM THE MUD

City lights shining across the night sky
Mask the gun smoke of everyday life
Blood in the streets, gun shells on the sidewalks
No one but us hear the screams

Of another lost friend, brother after brother
Silence fills the air with despair of another
Knowing that there is no way out of here
Many cars and faces passing through, but never stop to see

The real struggles of life, the deaths of young and bright futures
Sons and daughters of the next generation
Who's lives never could get started
Desperation everywhere, around every corner,
See, right here, meals are no guarantee
Shelter and a place to call home is almost nonexistent
Again no one ever cares to acknowledge the lives we live in the mud
There is no coping, no adjusting to blood filled streets, drug filled skies,
Knowing that every second could be your very last breath

Ever gone a week without even a piece of bread?
Ever gone a week without a glass of water?
Ever seen someone shot and killed in front of your very own eyes?
Ever had to kill someone to save your own life?

There is no just deal with it and move on where we come from
You just have to survive, pray and hope that you're not the next victim.
As you grow from these streets, if you survived,
you will have to separate yourself from the ones who made it,
and the ones fighting to make it.
For we are stronger than those who've already made it
and we are going further than they are.
We put our cities on our backs, for it is the reason we're here today,
The reason we will never go back there until mission complete

From the mud we have come,
for we have been stripped and torn,

our hearts and souls have been ripped from us,
our minds shattered and our blood drained beyond death.
We come to take back which has been taken from us,
We come to fight this endless war of life
We will never go back, We will never quit,
And We will never settle for less.

Here We come world,
we have fire in our eyes, ice in our veins, and iron in our hearts
For We have come from the mud
And are on our way to the top and beyond.

--Zachary Corrothers

THESE STREETS

Cold in the air, whispers in the wind
Disappointment all around, despair everywhere
Blood, sweat, and tears
This is how I got ice in my veins

I've got my city on my shoulders
Knowing these streets got my back
Failure and losses ain't getting any older
Cuz within these streets we don't get any slack

Pain, sickness, and death in our eyes
Weakness, withering in our hearts
In the darkness and shadows we hear all the cries
In these streets is where real strength starts

Grinding through the sorrow
Living like there is no tomorrow
Getting back up to your knees
Over and over til we feel free

Letting in the light, shining through
Giving us the sign of the immortal truth
That He never left us alone
And He, too, took every stone

For we call His name, Jesus
And these streets give Him the nod.
Humility and wisdom has become our creed
And In God We Trust indeed.

These streets have never lost hope
Searching and seeking out any answers to cope
Knowing it ain't about triumph
But about overcoming our failures

The angels watch over us on these streets
Bringing the thunder and the lightning to the streets

PERSEVERE

Igniting all of our hearts desires
Providing the passion we need to start the fire

And to keep the flames burning
Grunting and screaming continues churning
Perseverance and knowledge is our earning
Giving all the glory to God for the yearning.

Brotherhood, a family made of steel
Iron sharpening iron beneath our feet
Always reminding us of the feeling
When victory through God finally came in these streets.

-Zachary Corrothers

THE FLEETING

Grunting, yelling, screaming
These are things you hear dreaming
But what are they meaning
Blood, sweat, and tears--all part of the redeeming

Time and time again we are bleeding
Forgetting all of the needing
Of our hearts desires screaming
Humility and courage are fleeting

Cuz we have besieged our eyes lusting
After the things that leave us so untrusting
While hoping we always find the easy way out of something
But are burying ourselves deeper and deeper til we become nothing

And now scarred so far we are kneeling
Seeking any kind of healing
Searching for the voice of reason
Telling yourself is this the real thing or just another feeling?

--Zachary Corrothers

INVINCIBLE

Going through hell sounds more like a dream
Of the reality that broke me down to my knees
That destroyed every part of my heart and soul, it was the death of me,
As it consumed everything I thought I once believed.

It can't even compare to the real horror
That stripped me apart through terror
Not just once, but a thousand times over
Making me the slave of a pain bearer

Once I could stand within the flames of the fire
My transformation into the invincible was my desire
For I had been ripped into pieces and stripped beyond tire
Only now can I become that fire

It brought me back to my feet
To live, to stand up against the world's deceit
For now I know the pains of defeat
And am no longer among the weak

Because only with God am I Invincible

-Zachary Corrothers

THE FIGHT

Thought I had reached the top
Finding out I couldn't be more wrong,
Just like a bad flop
Truth is I am always climbing the endless mountain so why should I
stop?
While grinding is the name of the game,
the game itself is just the cream of the crop.

Hard work, determination, this is my solemn promise--my motivation.
A bleeding heart, a sweat-soaked body, and tear-filled eyes is my
provocation
Just me against me, staring into the eyes of the beast--my inspiration.
For the end result is not my concern, but the journey as my standing
ovation.

Bringing on the impossible, taking it head on
Lowering my shoulders, digging deep setting my own tone
Running right through the unbelievers, sending them all home
Relenting courage and strength while enduring every stone.

Never succumbing to the false prophets--the cowards of defeat.
Walking tall, head held high and standing on my own two feet
Overcoming the noise of the judges, never taking a seat
While moving forward is my only option, to be just part of the
victorious feat

Bringing others together, uniting a brotherhood of warriors with one
heart beat
Leading them to battle, rising up against any other fleet
And withstanding the world's greatest heat
Pushing and pulling til mission complete.

Crowds all around, raising the atmosphere
Noise surrounding the air, making the despair disappear
Forgetting all the failures and losses that bred eternal fear
Transforming hearts from the blind and lost to that of the found and
clear.

PERSEVERE

Deeper and deeper do I have to shovel to give my whole heart
Thinking the end is near would not be smart
Instead I believe no matter what I will survive every part
For this fight is my work of art.

-Zachary Corrothers

TESTAMENT OF COURAGE

The testament of courage
Is not about letting yourself get buried
By all the struggles of everyday life
Even if you sometimes have to succumb to the merciless knife

But to just stay ahead of the game
So others will know you walk without shame
Dedicating yourself to live beyond the fame,
Beyond the fortune, while enduring all of the pain

Living in the shadows of the light
Beneath the darkness before you can begin to take flight
Making yourself the flame that will ignite
Your passion to burn endlessly into the night

The testament of courage
Is not about using guns and bullets
But taking those bullets, selflessly,
For those that don't truly deserve it.

Courage under sparkling fires
Will be your desire
And the world will know that you're no liar
For now they've seen you come out from the mire

Determination, resonance, and perseverance,
This is my solemn promise to live by
A warrior's creed that I will cry
From now until the moment that I die.

-Zachary Corrothers

A NOTE FROM THE AUTHOR

The final piece from this Volume was written during a very tough time as my dad had been battling Stage IV Lung cancer and his chemo treatments only made him worse. And just before Christmas of that year, in 2010, I started writing each line of this poem. After each stanza, I started feeling much different about how things would end for my dad. Then, I began seeing a different look in his eyes; he had that warrior's look in his eyes, like he would not be defeated. Finally, the unthinkable had happened on Christmas Eve while meeting with his doctors. They could not explain it, but the cancer had fully disappeared. God showed his mercy by reaching into my dad's heart and helped him remember to continue the fight, then healed him. The experience was very rough and sorrowful, yet it showed me that no matter what life throws at you, take it head on, but win or lose, never back down without a fight.

NEVER BACKING DOWN

The weight gets heavier,
the sky grows darker,
And the nights are longer.
But I won't back down.

Stood here a thousand times before,
Stared in my eyes a million more,
Wore this groove into the ground.
No, I won't back down.

Doubt and pain, I call my friends,
Here from the beginning,
With me to the end.
They know I won't back down.

In the shadows, I've found the light.
Found my courage, found my fight.
In the darkness I have sight.
I won't back down, for the end is bright.

A warrior's creed that I cry,
a solemn oath to live by,
from this moment now, till I die...
I will never back down.

--Zachary Corrothers

THANK YOU TO MY READERS

Coming Soon…the second installment of the Never Give Up series, Resilient, will be another great collection of pieces of art focused on the art and science of bouncing back from adversities and failures. Be on the lookout for more of this incredible, inspiring series created and written by the author.

MORE FROM THIS AUTHOR

Coming Soon…the second installment of the Never Give Up series, Resilient, will be another great collection of pieces of art focused on the art and science of bouncing back from adversities and failures. Be on the lookout for more of this incredible, inspiring series created and written by the author.

Also Coming Soon…the first installment of the Love & Joy series, This Is Love, will be a collection of romantic love, brotherly and sisterly love, and self-love creations of art from this author. These poems will be great to share with a significant other, a best mate, or even use these to focus on loving thyself more. Remember, in order to give love to another, you must first learn to love yourself. So, be on the lookout for this amazing series on Amazon and Kindle.

NOTES

The keys to success lie
not within the tangible
but only can be
acquired through an
abstract view.